Heavenly Senses

By Danielle Bunkley
Illustrations by Madelein Terreros

TEACH Services, Inc.
PUBLISHING

World rights reserved. This book or any portion thereof may not be copied or reproduced in any form or manner whatever, except as provided by law, without the written permission of the publisher, except by a reviewer who may quote brief passages in a review.

The author assumes full responsibility for the accuracy of all facts and quotations as cited in this book. The opinions expressed in this book are the author's personal views and interpretations, and do not necessarily reflect those of the publisher.

This book is provided with the understanding that the publisher is not engaged in giving spiritual, legal, medical, or other professional advice. If authoritative advice is needed, the reader should seek the counsel of a competent professional.

Copyright © 2014 Danielle Bunkley
Copyright © 2014 TEACH Services, Inc.
ISBN-13: 978-1-4796-0358-9 (Paperback)
ISBN-13: 978-1-4796-0359-6 (iPad)
ISBN-13: 978-1-4796-0360-2 (Kindle Fire)
Library of Congress Control No: 2014940099

Published by

TEACH Services, Inc.
PUBLISHING
www.TEACHServices.com • (800) 367-1844

Dedication:

To my mom who inspires me daily, and to my students whom I can't wait to meet at the gate of Benjamin in heaven.

In heaven I want to hear Jesus laugh, see God on His throne, taste fruit from the tree of life, smell fresh clean air, touch a lion's mane, and meet Job, Moses, Enoch, Queen Esther, the woman who touched the hem of Jesus' garment …

In heaven I will see a shiny golden street where I can run and skip with my new pair of feet.

Revelation 21:21

In heaven I will see an eagle land on a giraffe, such amazing wonderful things, will really make me laugh.

Job 8:21

In heaven I will **hear** the angel choir that sings, and I will fly around with my new pair of wings.

1 Corinthians 2:9

In heaven I will *hear* the monkeys loudly *screeech*. I can hold them on my lap while I hear Jesus teach!

Mark 6:34

In heaven I will smell a red rose so big and fair. I'll take it to my grandma; I can't wait to see her there!

1 Thessalonians 4:16-17

In heaven I will smell orange and apple trees. I'll never get sick there, blow my nose, or even sneeze!

Revelation 21:4

In heaven I will **taste** the sweetest grapes or figs around. I'll dig up some fresh peanuts, or potatoes underground!

Revelation 19:17

In heaven I will *taste* a big orange carrot and a beet, and friendly bees will share their yummy honey, which is oh so sweet.

Leviticus 20:24

In heaven I can touch a big old grizzly bear. He won't try to bite when I scratch his fuzzy hair!

Isaiah 11:6

In heaven I will touch the scar on Jesus' hand. I'll ask what it is from; His love I'll understand.

John 3:16-17

In heaven I will learn about God's building plans. And there I'll find my mansion built by His own hands.

John 14:1-3

In heaven I will sit on Jesus' lap. I'll never feel tired or need a nap.

Revelation 21:23-25

In heaven I will wear a robe that's snowy white. Nothing there will hurt me; no dog will ever bite!

Revelation 3:5

In heaven I will wear a crown that will not bend. I cannot wait to get there. How 'bout you, my friend?

1 Peter 5:4/James 1:12

# In heaven I want to see.....

(draw what you want to see)

In heaven I will hear.....

(draw what you want to hear)

In heaven I will taste....

(draw what you want to taste)

 # In heaven I will smell....

(draw what you want to smell)

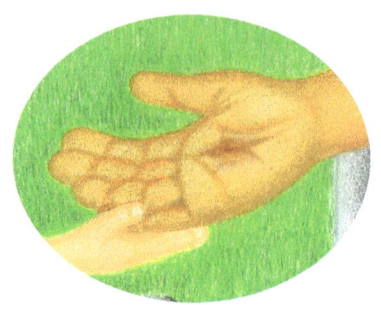 # In heaven I will touch...

(draw what you want to touch)

In heaven I want to meet...

We invite you to view the complete
selection of titles we publish at:

www.TEACHServices.com

Scan with your mobile
device to go directly
to our website.

Please write or e-mail us your praises, reactions, or
thoughts about this or any other book we publish at:

P.O. Box 954
Ringgold, GA 30736

info@TEACHServices.com

TEACH Services, Inc., titles may be purchased in bulk for
educational, business, fund-raising, or sales promotional use.
For information, please e-mail:

BulkSales@TEACHServices.com

Finally, if you are interested in seeing
your own book in print, please contact us at

publishing@TEACHServices.com

We would be happy to review your manuscript for free.

www.ingramcontent.com/pod-product-compliance
Lightning Source LLC
Chambersburg PA
CBHW081926170426
43200CB00014B/2850